LIFE SKILLS

I0895107

Neatness

Written by
Steffi Cavell-Clarke

KidHaven
PUBLISHING

Published in 2027 by
KidHaven Publishing, an Imprint of Greenhaven Publishing, LLC
2544 Clinton St., Buffalo, NY 14224

© 2026 BookLife Publishing Ltd.

Written by: Steffi Cavell-Clarke
Edited by: Beth Latham
Designed by: Rob Delph

All facts, statistics, web addresses, and URLs in this book were verified as valid and accurate at time of writing. No responsibility for any changes to external websites or references can be accepted by either the author or publisher.

Cataloging-in-Publication Data

Names: Cavell-Clarke, Steffi.
Title: Neatness / Steffi Cavell-Clarke.
Description: Buffalo, NY : KidHaven Publishing, 2027. | Series: Life skills | Includes glossary and index.
Identifiers: ISBN 9781534570610 (pbk.) | ISBN 9781534570627 (library bound) | ISBN 9781534570634 (ebook)
Subjects: LCSH: Orderliness--Juvenile literature. | House cleaning--Juvenile literature. | Cleanliness--Juvenile literature.
Classification: LCC BJ1533.O73 C349 2027 | DDC 648.5--dc23

All rights reserved.
No part of this book may be reproduced in any form without permission in writing from the publisher, except by a reviewer.

Printed in China

CPSIA compliance information: Batch #QS27KH: For further information contact Greenhaven Publishing LLC at 1-844-317-7404.

Please visit our website, www.greenhavenpublishing.com.
For a free color catalog of all our high-quality books, call toll free 1-844-317-7404 or fax 1-844-317-7405.

Find us on

Image Credits

Images courtesy of Shutterstock.com, unless otherwise stated.
Cover and recurring – Trzykropy, sunlight7, Johnny Dream, YummyBuum, Colorfuel Studio, ChipVector, Sudowoodo. 2–3 – Igisheva Maria. 4–5 – New Africa, Roman Samborskyi, ChipVector, YummyBuum, Beibeinside. 6–7 – New Africa, Klem Mitch. 8–9 – Seeme, Dmytro Zinkevych, Colorfuel Studio. 10–11 – Ovsiienko Mariia, Igisheva Maria. 12–13 – wavebreakmedia, PeopleImages, yulsiart. 14–15 – Natallia Ramanouskaya, Evgeny Atamanenko, ChipVector. 16–17 – Stephanie Frey, HalynaRom, Sudowoodo. 18–19 – New Africa, Jacob Lund, YummyBuum. 20–21 – New Africa, Thanakorn.P, Katja.Vary.Art. 22–23 – Studio Romantic, Beibeinside.

Contents

Words that look like this can be found in the glossary on page 24.

Let's Learn Life Skills!

Everybody learns life skills as they grow up. These skills help you become a helpful, happy person. Life skills help with things you do every day, such as keeping clean, playing with others, and staying safe.

Learning how to clean up is a part of growing up. It helps to keep your space clean, safe, and easy to use. It may feel like a boring job to do, but there are lots of ways to make it fun!

What Is Neatness?

We can all make a mess sometimes when we are busy enjoying ourselves. But it's important to clean up afterward so our space stays safe and ready for the next time we use it.

Neatness means putting things back where they belong so that everything is easy to find. A neat space can also help your mind feel calm and ready to play, learn, or relax.

Making Your Bed

A great way to start the day is by making your bed. It might seem like a small job, but it can make a big difference! Making your bed means you will have a neat, clean, and cozy bed to get into at bedtime.

All you need to do to make your bed is straighten out your pillow and blankets. Maybe you can put a cuddly toy on top to snuggle later.

Clean Up Your Toys

Have you ever stepped on a plastic block? Or slipped over a cuddly toy? It is important to clean up your toys after you've finished using them so you don't end up tripping over them!

CHOOSE IT, USE IT, PUT IT AWAY.

Toys can go into baskets, boxes, or bins. If everything has its own special place, then it will be easier for you to find them again. This means you will have more time to play with your toys.

Clean Up Your Books

Have you ever been inside a library? In a library, books are kept neatly on shelves. Each book has its spine facing out so you can easily see what it is called. This helps you to find the book that you are looking for quickly.

You can keep your books neat at home too. Taking care of your books means you can enjoy reading them again and again. Always remember to put books back on the shelf when you are finished.

Clean Up Your Clothes

Cleaning up your clothes helps keep your room neat and easy to move around in. Your clothes should be folded and put away or hung up in a closet to keep them clean and neat.

Dirty clothes go into the <u>laundry</u>. This means they can be washed and made ready for you to wear again. Taking care of your clothes shows you are growing up and being <u>responsible</u>.

Putting Away Your Coats and Shoes

After you have been playing outside, it is a good idea to hang up your coat and take off your shoes right away. This will stop any mud or dirt from coming inside your home.

Taking off your shoes keeps your floors clean and safe to walk on. Putting things away helps keep your home clean too. But don't worry if you get mud on the floor. You can always clean it up.

Clean Up Cups and Plates

There are often lots of dirty cups, plates, and <u>cutlery</u> after mealtimes. It's important to clean them and put them away to keep <u>germs</u> and bad smells away.

You can help wash up the dishes in the sink with warm, soapy water. Some houses have a dishwasher where you can neatly stack cups, plates, and cutlery. It will wash them for you.

Teamwork

Sometimes, a mess can seem so big that you don't know where to start. It is always OK to ask for help when you feel overwhelmed. An adult or a friend might be able to help.

Teamwork makes cleaning up faster and more fun! When everyone helps, the job gets done quicker. You can share tasks, encourage each other, and feel proud of working together as a team.

Making Cleaning Fun!

Sometimes cleaning can seem boring, but there are plenty of ways to make it fun!

You can listen to fun music or sing to get you motivated.

You can dance while you clean!

You can set a timer and see how much you can clean in 5 minutes.

You can have a race to see who can clean the fastest.

After you have finished cleaning, you can sit back and relax!

Glossary

CUTLERY	knives, forks, and spoons
ENCOURAGE	to give someone an idea or the confidence to do something
GERMS	tiny living things that can cause illnesses
LAUNDRY	the process of washing and cleaning clothes
MOTIVATED	feeling excited and ready to do something
OVERWHELMED	having too many things to do at once
RESPONSIBLE	in charge of doing certain things
SPINE	the edge of a book that shows its title

Index